To: ShiKera

With
Love & Healing,

Beth
Freeman

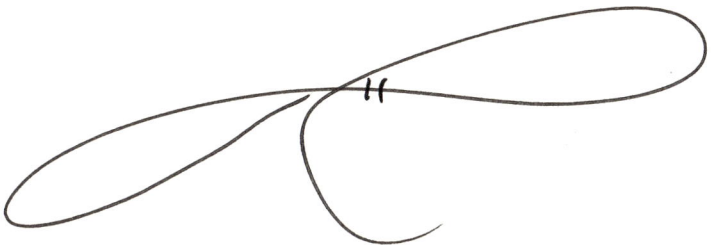

Forgiveness
for the
Soul

The Five Steps to Self-Forgiveness

Beth Freeman

BALBOA.PRESS
A DIVISION OF HAY HOUSE

Balboa Press books may be ordered through booksellers or by contacting:

Balboa Press
A Division of Hay House
1663 Liberty Drive
Bloomington, IN 47403
www.balboapress.com
844-682-1282

Print information available on the last page.

ISBN: 979-8-7652-2771-8 (sc)
ISBN: 979-8-7652-2770-1 (e)

Balboa Press rev. date: 05/11/2022

You want to perform a miracle? Forgive yourself.
–Rune Lazuli

Contents

Preface

Why write a book on forgiveness, particularly self-forgiveness? Because what I know to be true is that without self-forgiveness, we will continue to struggle with self-love. On my healing journey, I discovered that the true path to peace in my heart and love of myself came when I forgave myself for the choices I've made in this lifetime: choices that have hurt me, choices that have hurt others, and choices that will continue to harm until I let them go. It is when I began to forgive myself, truly forgive myself, that I began to heal. I found a strength I think I always knew I had, but with self-forgiveness I felt deserving of my own abilities. I discovered that my soul's purpose in life is helping others to heal and grow. I discovered that feeling one's own worth and value comes when we look at the duality of our shadows and our light, our challenges and our gifts, our weaknesses and our strengths. We must look at the entirety of ourselves. And by looking at ourselves so closely, we can't help but look at those situations, decisions, words, actions, and reactions that we hold shame around. It is in the releasing of shame that we find there is forgiveness of ourselves.

Yes, we can forgive others. Yes, others can forgive us. But the most powerful forgiveness of all is the forgiveness we give to ourselves. It is the language of self-love, and it is why we are here: to heal from our past, to learn to love ourselves, and to serve others with our gifts.

I am often asked, "What exactly is it you do?" I am a soul's purpose channeler. This is what I know to be true. I channel your personal guides and angels along with other light beings from a place of unconditional love and without judgment. Your guides only want what you desire deep within your own soul, and their purpose is to help you get there and find your own purpose through love and not fear. I am blessed to be a channel for one's personal guides and angels, and I am blessed to witness firsthand others heal and grow.

Early on, I set my intention that this work be only for healing, soul growth, or the greater good, and it continues to be just that. I am open to working with anyone who is seeking consistent awareness, exploration, and expansion to find his or her soul's purpose. I am living my soul's purpose, which is to help others heal, grow, and do the same. As a wonderful mentor of mine once said, "You cannot lead others down a path you have not yet walked yourself," and I know this to be true. I am a continued work in progress.

I have walked this path for decades and will continue to walk the path of truth as best I can, continuing to find the peace that flourishes where authenticity resides. Therefore, the words in these pages about my own personal journey may surprise or even disgust you, but most of all it is my hope that they empower you to forgive yourself. For we are all human beings, and as human beings we are imperfect, perfectly imperfect. We are the totality of ourselves—our shadows and our light—and forgiving ourselves is possible by accepting and loving all of ourselves. The steps to self-forgiveness are a very important part of that journey to peace and to love, and it is a gift we can give ourselves. Self-forgiveness is the ultimate act of self-love.

Some passages in this book are from my previous book, *Daylight for the Soul* (2017/2021). Please feel free to message me directly at everydaypeaceandpurpose.com, as I look forward to hearing from any who are searching or in need of guidance and love without judgment.

In love and light,
Beth

Introduction

Forgiveness is simply about loving, accepting, and letting go. One foundational truth about forgiveness is that it is important to be aware that there is always choice. Forgiveness is a choice, and it is easily forgotten that we can make the choice to forgive. A second foundational truth is that forgiveness is always about the person forgiving—whether you are forgiving yourself or another person, it is always about you. It is about how important it is to recognize that forgiveness is an act of love, an act of self-love; again, whether it be forgiving someone else or forgiving yourself. It is always an act of self-love to forgive. Carrying around the negative emotion that attaches to what there is to forgive, particularly with yourself, is carrying around the weight of compounded guilt and shame. It wears you down emotionally, mentally, physically and spiritually.

Forgiveness is lifting off the weight—the coat, so to speak—of guilt, regret, or shame about someone else or even yourself. Forgiveness is shedding the skin of the past. Forgiveness is letting the past go. Forgiveness is the path, the only path to peace. Everything else one does to lead to peace will cease—will stop at the door of forgiveness. One must find peace in the letting go of the hope that the past could be different, in accepting that the past cannot be changed, in understanding that no matter what occurred anything and everything a human being experiences or does or says is worthy of forgiveness.

What is forgiveness? It is loving oneself and loving one's fellow man, with the understanding that as humans we hurt ourselves and we hurt others. It is a cycle—a cycle that will continue until one soul forgives, and then in their forgiveness another soul forgives, and so on and so on and so on. The language of love or self-love is forgiveness, simply and absolutely. Every human soul must understand that the experiences in your life, both positive and negative, are for your own soul's evolution. Everything in your life is all in divine order, even the pain, even the trauma, even the suffering—all of it is for your soul to learn and to grow. This is a necessary piece of forgiveness. Think of it this way: to know that it is for your own healing and soul growth can make it easier to accept, to let go, and to forgive.

Understanding soul contracts can also be helpful in forgiving others as well as forgiving oneself. Simply stated, when a soul chooses lessons for a lifetime, there are agreements or contracts with other souls to help learn the lessons chosen for one's lifetime. It is to understand on a deeper level how one can forgive someone's abuse, for example, by truly seeing the sacrifice of another soul as a contract in one's life to be an abuser. In turn, the abused soul can learn from and move into a space of gratitude for what happened because the trauma and what followed led the abused soul to find its purpose and its peace. This can take months to years of healing work, so to simplify it becomes difficult.

How can we simplify something so vast? How can we simplify what can be truly overwhelming? Through love and the understanding that pain and trauma are the building blocks of the soul, and removing these blocks is key to the awareness of love within. From a place of love, your soul shows you the lessons of this lifetime. Believe and have faith that every single experience you have had has led you closer and closer to the love within you.

Forgiveness does not come from any human being, other than your very own soul. No one else can absolve your guilt, no one else can take away your regret, and no one else can free you from your shame but you. You can speak the language of love, of pure love. Forgiveness is the language of divine love, the pure divine love that is within each and every one of you. Therefore, you *can* forgive yourself. Through love and forgiveness, you can accept and love yourself. Walk the path of forgiveness, walk the path to the love within you, and walk the path to peace within your heart and soul.

Peace

Peace is the prize. It is what all souls are striving for, whether they realize it or not. With peace comes happiness, with peace comes fulfillment, with peace comes love in all forms and in all ways. It is really peace you seek when you are looking for what has been lost. It is peace you seek when you are searching for the next best thing or setting your sights on something more, something better, but you just can't quite put your finger on it. It is peace.

Peace is the ultimate equalizer. It does not matter if you are rich or poor, what color your skin is, what religion you practice, or even if you don't practice at all. Peace is available to everyone. Peace is possible for everyone. With all the talk about peace in the world, doesn't it make sense to have peace individually first? Do you not think that if all the world's leaders had peace in their own souls, they would put an end to war? When peace is in individuals, then peace is in families. When peace is in families, then peace is in communities. When peace is in communities, then peace is in cities. When peace is in cities, then peace is in states. When peace is in states, then peace is in countries. When peace is in countries, then peace will be in the world. When there is peace in the world, there will be peace on the planet. When there is peace on the planet, then the universe will stop trying to get human attention, be it with natural disasters or famine or strife. There will be no need. There will be peace, and all will be well.

It sounds so simple, but it is true. If each and every human on the planet searched for peace within and worked toward that all-encompassing goal, there would be peace on the planet. Peace is possible one person at a time; peace is possible one soul at a time. Peace is possible because peace is possible in your soul. Today. Begin today to find peace, inner peace.

How, you ask? Peace comes from forgiveness, peace comes from letting go of the past, peace comes with understanding the past so that you can release it. Peace comes with forgiving yourself even more than you forgive others. Peace comes from allowing fear and all negative emotion from the past to leave so that more and more love takes its place. Peace is founded on the following acts: awareness, acceptance, understanding, ownership, and forgiveness of self. It begins and ends with you.

Be aware that you have wounds to heal; be aware that there is more to you, more for you in this life. Accept your perfect imperfections, and strive to understand the whys of your decisions, even those decisions you may regret. Own each thought, feeling, word, action, reaction, and any that hurt yourself or others or both. Ownership can be difficult, because there is no victim when you own what you said or didn't say, what you did or didn't do, and when you look at who you were with awareness, acceptance, and understanding—and you own it all. Then you will find the compassion to forgive who you were then and finally be at peace with yourself. Then, finding peace within yourself, you will look at others with more acceptance and understanding and will begin to see your place in how to bring peace to others. And so it goes, and so it goes. Peace: it is possible, it is probable, it is yours.

from *Daylight for the Soul* (2017/2021)

Chapter 1

Awareness

To be aware is necessary for the first step of self-forgiveness. You must know what is keeping you from peace. That peace can be found when you let go of the past and of that which is keeping you in a place of guilt, regret, shame, and the feeling that you are unworthy. It is simply being aware that what you're holding on to is not all in the present—it comes from the past, invades your present, and will be part of your future unless you release it.

The first stage of awareness is waking up – also known as awakening - to the fact that there is more to your life and that *something is going on*. You are not quite sure why it's happening or what it is, but you know that there is more for your soul's purpose than what you are currently doing and that there is more to life than this. Simply stated, you know you are awakening when your life feels false, you crave meaning and purpose, you feel lost and alone at times yet crave solitude, you see through the illusions of society, you begin to experience more synchronicity, and you feel deeper empathy and compassion toward other beings.

Somehow, some way, guilt, regret, shame, and other negative emotions rooted in fear are coming up, and you are unsure why. When you want to understand what is happening that is the second stage of awareness. When you become aware of the past coming up in the present, then you must look inside and do the work to figure out what is coming up and more importantly, why it is coming up.

When you become aware that the negative emotions you feel are about something from the past that is the third stage of awareness. When negative emotions from the past come into the present, they can feel insurmountable because they can be so overwhelming. You realize that not only are you still carrying the past with you into the present, but the past is also keeping you from finding true joy in this life. Your past regret, past guilt, and past shame are keeping you from feeling at peace in the present. This awareness will lead you down the path of self-forgiveness, and this path will lead you to understanding yourself so much more. As a result, you will be able to fully accept and love yourself.

The five stages of awareness are:

1. waking up – also known as an awakening
2. wanting to understand why you are waking up and what you are waking up to
3. acknowledging you feel negative emotions such as guilt, regret, and/or shame that may be coming up from the past
4. realizing that you have the power to forgive yourself for past actions
5. understanding that you are ready to take the steps necessary to heal, to let go, and to find your purpose in this life

What does awareness actually look like, and how do you know you're finally aware? The human brain has an amazing capacity to protect the individual. As a matter of fact, the ego's main function is to protect you at all costs—even if that cost is your own peace and your own happiness. We get caught up in the patterns of our lives—the soul contracts that we have—and the ego-self is all about fear and how to cope with fear. Fear is the result of pain and suffering that all human beings encounter while living a human life. The coping skills you learn in response to fear can make you think you are dealing with your life, but under close observation, many of these coping skills are unhealthy and do not necessarily address the origin of the fear itself. When you wake up, you become aware that this fear inside you is somehow also rooted in the past. Awareness is all about recognizing that the present is not the only thing hurting you.

No matter what you have chosen to go through in the early parts of your life, all experiences leave indelible prints on you. On the inside, you are every age you have ever been, and every age within you has emotions, particularly negative emotions, that were not able to be to be shared or felt because you were told not to feel them, you didn't know how to feel them, or you simply pushed them down. It is these suppressed emotions that come up when you are ready to heal the wounds of the past and become aware that there is something to heal.

Awareness is not a step to work through quickly, even though it seems like it would be. Your ego-mind is there to protect you, which means it's also there to keep you from the truth. When the truth hurts you, terrifies you, or is too much to bear, your mind will protect you from the truth. Awareness is discovering the truth; awareness is figuring out that there is more to be known and that no, pushing it down does not work. Awareness brings you one step closer to forgiveness of self.

My Personal Journey to Awareness

I don't think I was aware that I had anything to forgive within myself for years. I was in full-on victim mode. I blamed everyone and everything for the choices I made. When everything came to light in my memory of my father and his abuse of me, I knew there was a lot of blame, and I, the victim part of me, felt entitled: "I am entitled to this because you did this and you did that." With my father and my mother, particularly, I felt entitled to spend their money. They didn't have a lot, but they had some, and at the time I believed that they owed me. I had that awareness long before I had an awareness of doing something that I felt ashamed of, because over the years, I would justify it every which way I could in my mind. The truth is, I stole from my parents by manipulating them to get money. I justified it with such thoughts as, *Well, I'm taking care of them. I'm helping them. I'm the one that's doing all this for them.* However, that was my choice and again, the feeling that they owed me came from a place of entitlement.

I did not realize there was something to forgive, even after my brother said some hard truths about my behavior at the time. I still felt entitled. However, it did make me aware that there was something I was doing wrong, and to be frank, I knew that I was taking from them. I knew that all along. So there was awareness but not necessarily the awareness that is necessary for self-forgiveness, because I was still blaming someone other than myself. I was still not ready to face my shame. Until I was at a point where I was truly aware that I had shame for my actions and understood why I acted this way, I was not ready to forgive myself. I was still in pain and felt my actions were justified, even as I was facing the consequences of my actions. Those consequences led me to an awareness of my shame; I realized there was something to forgive.

For me, the consequences of my actions and the entitlement I felt eventually led me down a path to two bankruptcies—a Chapter 7 and a Chapter 13. I felt a little bit better about the one I paid back; however, I will never forget seeing my consequences and my subsequent shame laid out before me. In bankruptcy court, there was a man, an entrepreneur, who had done some work around the house. He had his own landscape design company and didn't have a lot of capital. I believe all I owed him was $186, but I included him in my bankruptcy, and he came to bankruptcy court to try to get that money. I remember facing him and feeling the shame wash over me. Another time, I got called into court for not paying back a payday loan (which led to the second bankruptcy). I was before the judge, and he read the document that I had signed agreeing to 459 percent interest. He said my name, then he said, "Ma'am, I simply cannot save you from yourself." Another time, a debt collector showed up at the school where I taught to find me and get me to pay back a loan. Then there was the time that my car transmission went out, and I sobbed uncontrollably over not having the cash or the credit to fix my car—so much so that the mechanic loaned me his truck so I would have a car to drive, and a dear friend stepped in to help pay for it and allowed me to pay her back over time.

These experiences of shame around money and my mishandling of it really stemmed from a place of entitlement. Entitlement is just one form of victimhood. Awareness came when I recognized the victim inside me and the shame I truly felt. I became aware that I had made choices that I was ashamed of and that I regretted, and that's where I began the path to self-forgiveness.

So awareness truly is the first step to self-forgiveness, because if we don't feel like we've done anything wrong, or we justify what we've done, then we lack awareness. Without awareness, the rest of the steps don't matter. The other steps can be done out of order; it's not critical to do them in order. However, I've come to know that awareness is first and foremost, because if I don't think there's anything that I must forgive myself for, or nothing comes to mind, or if I justify it and make excuses for it, I'm not ready to forgive myself yet—not until I feel the guilt, regret and/or shame and know it is me and only me who has made the choice. That becomes the critical tipping point for awareness. Awareness that I have something within me to forgive and now am ready to move further on the path of self-forgiveness to acceptance.

Acceptance

Why is it so difficult to accept yourself for who you are? Why is it that you seek acceptance from everyone around you, yet sometimes fail to seek it from the most important person— you? The only acceptance you need is the acceptance of your own heart, your own mind, your own body, your own soul. That is all. Accept and love yourself for who you are, and you will no longer seek acceptance outside yourself. Acceptance, gratitude, and love can all be found within.

Remember, any positive emotion found from within can never be taken from you, and it is not dependent on anything external. The way to acceptance and the way to self-love is from within. Begin by accepting that which is easiest to accept and believe. Maybe it is your natural talent, maybe it is your intelligence, maybe it is your athleticism, maybe it is your creativity, maybe it is your sense of humor, maybe it is your work ethic, maybe it is your health—whatever it is, accept what is easy to accept first. Then this acceptance can be built upon, layer by layer, as you look deep within at who you are—who you *really* are. Not how others see you, but how you see yourself.

How do you talk to yourself? Do you say kind words about yourself, or are you self-critical? Self-criticism will do more damage to the soul than any words from another. Why? Because your own words never leave you until you let them go. They will play through your mind and your heart and your soul forever if you let them. It is up to you to silence the words of self-doubt, self-loathing, and self-hatred and replace them with words of encouragement, acceptance, and love.

Again, start with what you truly believe is worthy of acceptance. Each and every soul is equipped with gifts and strengths that are brought into this lifetime just for times when they are needed most. Take the time to evaluate who you are and what makes you unique and what is easy to accept about yourself. Begin at the beginning, and one by one begin to accept each and every part of yourself. Then you may get to the place where you can no longer accept yourself, and where the negative and hurtful words come in, and you feel lost and abandoned and unlovable. This is where healing is needed, and this is where you can begin.

The path to acceptance begins with that which you find unacceptable. That which you cannot stand about yourself. That which you find unlovable. This is where you begin healing, and healing will bring you to acceptance, and acceptance will bring you to love, and love will bring you to peace. Begin healing today and find your way to accept, love, and be at peace with all the parts of you—not just the strengths and gifts, but your weaknesses and shadows too. They are all a part of you and must eventually be accepted and loved in order for you to find the peace you seek.

from *Daylight for the Soul* (2017/2021)

Chapter 2

-⸱⟨⸱ ⟩⟨⟨ ⟨⸱⟩⸱-

Acceptance

Acceptance in the art of forgiveness is accepting that the past is the past and cannot be changed. You can change all the scenarios you fantasize about—you can imagine how life would be different if you could interweave different people, different souls, into the mix to change it. But the fact remains that the past cannot be changed or undone. Accept that you have made decisions from a place of pain and suffering, a place when you were without understanding, in a place and time that truly was in the past. For example, the child within: if every age you have ever been is within you, then some of the decisions you have made in your life that you feel guilt, regret, or shame around could have been led by the child within you. So, it is about accepting that not only am I who I am in this moment, I am every age I've ever been, and all my experiences I have ever had are within me.

With this acceptance that I am everything, I must learn to accept my own truth, my own experience, my own choices, and my own misdeeds. Acceptance comes in many forms. First is the acceptance that the past cannot be changed. Second is the acceptance of everything you have experienced, body, mind, heart, and soul. Third is accepting that these choices you made more than likely came from a place of pain, suffering, and not understanding the reasoning behind the decision. Fourth, acceptance is also accepting that you have a shadow side to yourself, that you are made of light, but with the light comes the shadow. You are a whole person with shadow and light, weaknesses and strengths, challenges and gifts.

As a whole person with shadow and light, you must accept your shadows—the sides of yourself that create shame and reasons to feel guilty or have regret. It is not only accepting your shadows; you have to understand them as well, but we will get to that later. But for now, it is enough to start by simply accepting the fact that you are a whole human being. You are a person who is made up of all your experiences in this life and beyond, not just years ago but minutes ago. Words that were said cannot be unsaid, actions that were taken cannot be taken back, reactions that were hurtful cannot be changed and cannot be removed from the memory of the other person or yourself—not truly.

So what is in this acceptance, this acceptance of self and of the whole being? It is accepting that the past cannot be changed no matter how hard you try. No matter how you try to fix, change, or remember it a different way, the past is the past and always will be. Learn from it, use it as a tool, but accept that it cannot be changed and accept the part you played in the narrative.

May these seven affirmations guide you on the path to your own acceptance.

1. I am made up of all experiences, emotions, and memories in this lifetime and beyond.
2. I am unable to take back, unsay, or change any words, actions, or reactions that happened before this very moment.

3. I accept that I am made up of good and bad, shadow and light; I will accept my weaknesses as much as I accept my strengths.

4. I will use this tool of acceptance to further my spiritual journey and move towards a place of accepting.

5. I am a spiritual being, having a human experience, and a human experience is inherently made of lessons to be learned.

6. I will learn the lessons of this lifetime, and I accept that my soul shows these lessons and that I chose my shadows and my light.

7. I choose to be a whole person in this lifetime, perfectly imperfect, and I will strive to accept exactly who I am in the present and who I become in the future.

My Personal Journey to Acceptance

Acceptance in self-forgiveness is not necessarily accepting what you did. You may still feel great shame around it. You may still know that it's something you wish you didn't do, but plain and simple, it's accepting the fact that you cannot change what has already occurred. You cannot take it back. For me, acceptance was difficult when it came to realizing that I could not change the way I chose to leave my husband and my child. Acceptance was hard for me because I wanted to change the narrative. I remember talking about it and making it sound like, "Oh, I didn't leave my husband for another man. I didn't have an affair." After all, I waited until divorce papers were signed to have sex with him. I was in full-on denial. I could justify it by saying I had just come to a realization about my father and his abuse of me as a child. More justification.

I made all these excuses to avoid accepting what I did as what it was. So, it's not just accepting that you can't change the past. It's accepting what you did realistically and not changing the narrative. And that's key, because if we feel shame around anything, we'd like to change the narrative around it. We'd like to change the story. We'd like to make it different. And we can't. And so, in my case, the acceptance obstacle was in how I left my husband, gave up primary custody of my son, and in effect just checked out of my family—my husband, my child, my parents. I really tried to change the narrative about the way I did it, make that narrative into something completely different that made me feel less shame.

It took a long time for me to accept that this is what I did, and it hurt others, including those I love. I would make all these excuses as to why I did what I did, but true acceptance came with me believing not only that I could not change the past, but that this is the reality of my past. You see, that's part of acceptance. It's both; you've got to have the reality match the circumstances. Otherwise, you're still in justification mode, not ready to accept your actions, let alone the consequences of those actions. When we are still justifying our actions, acceptance can be overlooked— it took me probably ten years after the fact even to apologize for my actions. I was working on so many other aspects of my healing and my growth, but I was not able to accept the true narrative, the truth, and express how I felt about it: shame.

I think I had already *understood*, which is a separate step (and this is where the steps of self-forgiveness don't always come in in order), why I did it, but I didn't accept the story as it truly was until much later. In acceptance, we are not only facing our shame, we are also accepting that we made these choices. I hurt others, and I hurt myself as well, but it was only when I accepted the truth that it was for all involved, I was able to move through the other steps of self-forgiveness.

I want to be clear that self-forgiveness does not require someone else forgiving you. It doesn't. As a matter of fact, I don't know whether my ex-husband has forgiven me to this day—and he doesn't ever have to, as that is his choice. I did not need his forgiveness or even my son's for me to accept my choices and move through the steps of self-forgiveness. That's why it's called *self-*forgiveness: it's accepting what I did and the reality of it. It isn't simply that I cannot change the past, but that I accept it as it was for all parties—not just for myself. I accepted the past as it was and began to heal my past through acceptance of myself in the present.

In learning the lessons of a lifetime and finding acceptance, we find true healing. In letting go of the past and our desire to change it, we heal and step into our own power. When we release the past, here are some ways we create space to let something else in.

We learn to let go of …	We replace it with …
self-judgment/condemnation	self-acceptance/self-love
shame/unworthiness	innocence/self-worth
being invisible/silent	allowing ourselves to be seen and heard
isolation/emotional disconnection	community/emotional connection
giving our power away	stepping into our power
blaming others	taking responsibility
judging others	looking at our triggers and our wounds
stuffing or running from our fear	being with our fear with compassion
pleasing others	honoring ourselves
controlling others	giving others permission to be themselves
being abused or controlled	saying no and setting boundaries
working for others	working with others
ignoring or disparaging our gifts	trusting and expressing our gifts
running away from love	acknowledging our fear of intimacy
attacking others	owning our anger and not projecting it
perfectionism	realistic expectations of self/others
addictive patterns	facing the pain behind them
lack of confidence	taking small steps/taking the pressure off
negativity	cultivating a positive attitude
blaming/attacking ourselves	forgiving/being gentle with ourselves

Chapter 3

———— ⁓ ❧ ⁓ ————

Understanding

Learn from the past, don't live there.
Ted Kills in the Fog, 2004 Sedona Retreat

The next step to self-forgiveness is understanding why you make decisions that hurt you or anyone else. Any regret, any reason for not being able to let go of the past, is an opportunity to understand. Understand the origin of your own pain so that you know why you inflict pain of any kind on yourself or another person. This psychic pain, if you will, is at the core of what is hurting all humanity. Simply put, when you hurt, you can choose to hurt either yourself or someone else. The way to stop the cycle of hurt and pain is the third step of self-forgiveness: understanding—not just knowing, but a true resonating *understanding* of the origin of the pain and the underlying reason for the behavior that happens in this lifetime.

This current lifetime begins before one is born. It begins with the soul contracts attached to the lessons a soul chooses to learn in this lifetime. These soul contracts are bound by each soul, and souls will serve their contracts well. Lessons are learned through adversity, pain, and suffering. How one learns to overcome pain and suffering sometimes comes through *causing* pain and suffering. It is not a conscious thought, necessarily; it is simply a human desire to compensate for what is missing, damaged, or perceived to be lost. You see, it is not actually lost—the light is within each and every soul on the planet, and that light will show the way to understanding.

In order to understand, you must first be aware and accept that there is more to this human life—that there is a greater good, that there is a team of souls looking out for each and every soul on the planet, and that there is help to be found. To understand is to believe that there are reasons, which are not the same as justifications, for doing the things we do. There are reasons for acting out or acting up, for saying or speaking words that hurt or for not speaking up when the truth could help someone. It is in the nature of doing or not doing that is key to understanding.

Understanding is the "why" of what one regrets in a lifetime, and without the why, the same patterns of behavior can and will continue until you stop and take the time to truly understand the origin of pain in your own life. The act of simply being a human being is painful. Stop the cycle of pain and of hiding that pain or acting out on it by taking the time and effort necessary to understand it.

To understand is not necessarily to relive the past, but you must remember it and walk through it with an open heart—open to understanding, open to believing, open to knowing that deep down inside there is always a reason, always a lesson, always a contract. The first soul contracts are with your parents. Each soul chooses parents for the lessons of that lifetime, and no matter how good or bad, loving or unloving parents may be, they are there to originate the first lessons of this lifetime.

This is not about going against your upbringing but understanding the soul contracts all souls have with their parents.

For example, did you choose this lifetime to be one of distrust? Did you choose a life in which it would be hard, if not almost impossible, to trust anyone—including yourself? Then does it not make sense that you would choose one or both parents to hurt or betray you in some way so that you could obtain the gift—yes, it is a gift—of learning to mistrust? Having experienced mistrust, you may one day wake up and realize that you want to know how to *trust* someone, that trust is missing from your life, and you will want to learn as much as you can so that you can trust others and in turn trust yourself.

If your soul chose abandonment or fear of abandonment to be a major lesson in this lifetime, then does it not make sense that you would choose one parent, or both, to abandon you through divorce, neglect, abuse, or even death? Realizing that you have important and loving soul contracts with your parents can help you apply the steps outlined within these pages so that you can mend relationships and forgive others—but as stated at the beginning, it is most important that you first forgive yourself.

Understanding is the third step to self-forgiveness. So how do you begin to understand?

First, recognize the soul contracts in your life, particularly the negative ones. As you know already, lessons are not usually learned from love—they are learned most definitely from fear and all negative emotion rooted in this fear. Once you have acknowledged those who have hurt you and the ways that you feel and process this hurt, then you can begin to allow the feelings of hurt, anger, resentment, sorrow, and pain to leave with each memory that comes up for you. You do not have to remember or relive everything painful from your life—only that which is necessary for understanding.

When you are ready to forgive yourself and have walked through awareness and acceptance, then you are ready to understand and release the memories that flow through you. Others in your life—the most intimate relationships you have, but also some not so close—will trigger the past to come up for you. When you are triggered, you will notice that your negative emotions are exaggerated or do not fit the situation at hand. This is how you know you are being triggered. In this state, you are likely reacting as a child or a younger version of yourself. Remember, every age you have ever been is inside you, and every memory is contained within, even if you are not conscious of it. You are already programmed to be triggered when you are ready to release the negative emotion. Working with a healer, or light worker, is very helpful during the understanding phase of self-forgiveness.

Your guides are ready to help you. They have been chosen by you before this lifetime and are with you from the onset, and they will be with you until the day you choose to go home. You can reach your guides on your own through meditation and automatic writing, and you can also access them more directly through a light worker, someone who has also walked this path of healing and has chosen to help others do the same in this lifetime. Light workers are on this planet to help everyone who is ready to understand and to move from a place of fear to a place of love.

Acceptance or love of self comes from understanding and is illuminated and made brighter by self-forgiveness. How can you own what you do not understand? In order to get to the fourth step of ownership, you must understand the soul contracts chosen, the lessons for what one is holding on to with regret or pain, and you must realize that all experiences of a life are important to healing and soul growth.

Take the time to understand the whys of your life so that you can release the negative emotion and negative energy contained within. This releasing frees up space for love to reside, for love to be felt, for love to be free. The freedom that comes with understanding is not to be taken lightly. It is life changing. To understand is to see the bigger picture of your life and at the same to see how all the parts fit together to make you exactly who you are in this moment. You are worthy of love and understanding, so give yourself the time and effort to understand your own motivations and your own pain.

My Personal Journey to Understanding

Understanding was—and still is—the longest and sometimes the most difficult process for me. To understand is not just theoretically understanding in my mind, it's understanding the multiple layers of my own behavior. It's understanding everything that I've experienced in this life, from the moment I entered my mother's womb to the present. It's every single age within me, every single experience I have encountered. In understanding how all these experiences work and come together, I can more fully understand why I made choices that hurt myself and others and have brought about shame in my life.

So understanding really does take me down a path beyond what there is to forgive within me. Understanding, for me, was key for my healing, and it has taken a long time. Just like an onion, I can peel the layers and keep peeling and peeling before I get to the core. So too with your heart and soul when you peel back the layers of everything that's happened in your life, the layers of every aspect of your life that has something to do with what is bringing you pain and shame.

That was a huge step for me, as I just had to understand whatever was bringing me pain and shame. Although I'm presenting understanding as the third step of self-forgiveness, in some ways it's the one that I started first. I sought help from an energy healer who is also a counselor, and without her help I don't think I could have done it as quickly as I did, even though it's taken years. There was so much buried between the layers that to this day I still work to get a better understanding of my life and the choices I've made.

I believe that understanding myself is a lifelong process but understanding why I made the choices I did (and sometimes still do) that hurt myself and others effectively brings me to this place of wanting to forgive myself. Understanding allows me the time and grace to unlock all the doors, unlock all the compartments where my pain and shame have lived. I compartmentalized so much of the pain that it took me a long time to get to it and to get to that understanding.

I learned that while I could forgive myself in small bits and pieces, or I could forgive big things, no matter what I am forgiving, I still have to figure out why—my why. And it's not as simple as my dad having abused me, or my mother having deep depression and leaving me emotionally. That's a reason, maybe, that abandonment was a trigger for me, or that I was always looking for love in sexual relationships, but it wasn't truly understanding myself. It was more that this is what happened to me, and it was more about trying to justify my actions.

Understanding my why became a journey, a journey into not only the past of my childhood, but the past of my teenage and my young adult years. It led to an understanding of why I chose the husband I did—someone who was very safe, who felt very safe to me. It led to an understanding of why I chose a career that I was told I would be "good at" instead of the career I had wanted all my life. Even then, there was so much shame building in my life that had nothing to do with the shame around being sexually abused—or so I thought. I created a life where I chose to do a lot of things that brought me shame. Whether it was making a grade lower than a B in school, or being caught stealing, or being promiscuous in college, or being fired multiple times in the career I was supposed to be "good at," I still couldn't get to the understanding of the root shame in my life: if I'm not lovable to the first people in my life who are there to love me, then not only do I not love myself, but anybody who loves me must have something wrong with them. Hence hurting my college boyfriend and hurting my husband because they both actually loved me, and then falling in love with men in between who were struggling to love themselves and whose lack of ability to love me I took as a sign that I could "save" them. I was always searching for love even when I had men in my life who did love me. I did not understand for a long time that it was about learning to love myself first. I was not creating self-love because of the way I treated others and what I did to hurt myself and bring about more shame.

I believe part of the understanding process around shame is recognizing that what we hide from others is one thing, but what we hide from ourselves is another. We can hide a lot from other people, but it becomes difficult to hide from our own shame. It will come out, and it will come out in ways that are self-harming and are hurtful to others because of the decisions we made. To truly understand ourselves, is to understand all these complicated feelings and the actions that come with them.

I can't say enough about the understanding process being in layers. For example, I believe that I can get to a place of self-forgiveness and still uncover more understanding about myself over time. So it isn't that I must understand every single nuance of myself at once; I can forgive myself in pieces. What was key for me is that once I passed through the steps of awareness and acceptance, I then could understand my reasons for my shame enough to begin seeking self-forgiveness.

I want to add here that sometimes understanding can come across a little bit like justification, and justification is most definitely not one of the stages of self-forgiveness. However, justification is a desire to explain the why, and that explanation can lead to knowing the true reason and reaching a new level of understanding. So when I sought self-forgiveness, I was able to focus my energy and intention: I want to understand why I did *this*—not X, Y, or Z, but A; I want to understand A, and if I can understand A, then I can get to B, C, and D; and so on. So I would focus on figuring out whatever was coming up for me at the time. Why did I do this? Why would I do that? And when I could answer from a knowing place within, I was ready for the next step of taking ownership of my choices and the decisions that led to my shame.

Chapter 4

Ownership

Once you understand why you have made the decisions you did, then you can begin the process—in fact, sometimes the most difficult step—of taking ownership of your own behavior and decisions. This is called responsibility. This is not a place of being the victim; this is the step where you let go of the attachment to victimhood and you take responsibility. Take complete ownership of your actions or inaction, including decisions you regret, and take ownership for hurting yourself or others—for anything that has not served your soul.

Ultimately it is in awareness, acceptance, and understanding that you can finally let go of the blame and find how empowering it is to *own* your life—not to put blame on others but rather to take ownership of the fact that you chose: "I did it of my own free will. I made the choice, and the choice I made may have hurt myself or someone else." This realization, however, is hard for all human beings. To be aware, to accept, to understand, and then to own the fact that yes, when we hurt, we hurt others. When we're hurt ourselves, we sabotage ourselves with unhappiness. It is part of human nature.

There are several archetypes that come into each lifetime regardless of the lessons chosen by that soul. Three of those archetypes that are prevalent in the need for self-forgiveness are the child, the saboteur and the victim. The child part of the healing process is allowing yourself to realize that some of your decisions were made by a much younger version of you, maybe a you from ten years ago, or your teenage or childhood self. Every human being plays the victim at one time or another, be it the victim of abuse or neglect, the victim of circumstance, or the victim of—well, we could go on and on, but everyone reading this can think of one time or another when you felt victimized in some way. It might be in your personal life or at work, but you know you have been.

Letting go of the victim archetype is to let go of being attached to the feeling that everything is beyond your control, and is a very important part of self-forgiveness. It empowers you to take complete ownership of everything that has occurred in your life, good and bad, knowing that you played a hand in everything every step of the way. This ownership is empowering! No longer are you the victim; no longer is it someone else's fault, something or someone outside of you—it now belongs to you. And yes, even if it's sometimes painful to look at it this way, to own the behavior empowers you to own your decisions and every part of your life.

This is where the saboteur comes in. When you do not feel worthy or deserving, you will sabotage something good in your life so that you can stay in the comfortable place of victimhood. This sabotage hurts you and others around you, depending on the circumstance. Ownership is understanding that your saboteur is at work each and every day, with that little nudge that you're not sure you're worthy of forgiveness. It's time to say goodbye to the saboteur. Ownership is empowering and allows the saboteur to go to sleep. This saboteur must no longer play a part in your life.

With awareness, acceptance, understanding, and now ownership, the saboteur has nothing to sabotage—because yes, you are worthy of living in a place of love and acceptance and peace. So how do you begin the process of ownership? Simply put, once you have understanding, then let that understanding go. It sounds somewhat counterproductive, does it not? But it is important to let go of the reasons why and to simply own your body, mind, and spirit. Ownership is necessary for self-awareness, self-acceptance, and ultimately self-love. It can be a difficult step to face your truth without any justification—simply ownership. It strips everything bare and allows you to be free—free of the victimhood, free of the saboteur—and it helps that child within you to go inside your heart and be understood, heard, and loved leading you to the next step of compassion.

My Personal Journey to Ownership

The fourth step of self-forgiveness is ownership. Ownership is one of those tricky, tricky words. Sure, I take ownership. Sure, I did it. But that is not ownership. I could have said that a billion times and not truly taken ownership for what I chose to do in my life that hurt myself and hurt others. I took ownership when I accepted and understood that I *chose* to hurt myself or others with no regard for anything else. That was the moment I owned my shadow self. Taking full ownership of my shadow self for me was the realization that entitlement had become part of my life in too many ways. I felt entitled to have others take care of me, I felt entitled to have others see my point of view, I felt entitled to get what I wanted, and I felt entitled to pretend or not pretend with others in my life.

When I began my second· career as a teacher—what I had wanted to be all my life—I cared very much for my students, especially those whose home lives were difficult. I found myself being more authentic with these amazing kids, teaching and helping them, and empowering them with their own self-confidence. That in turn helped me face the parts of myself that I absolutely hated. Teaching gave me not only the gift of doing something so natural to me, but also the strength to face the worst parts of myself— because ownership is facing the worst parts of yourself.

I am not going to sugarcoat it. It is easy to say, "I'll take ownership. I know I did it." It goes beyond that to, "I know I did it, and I knew what I was doing. I did it anyway, and I hurt others and I hurt myself, and I am truly seeking forgiveness." Taking ownership continues to this day. Some days I find myself wanting to change the narrative of my past, wanting to justify the decisions I made that hurt me and most of all hurt others. However, I still must own every bit of it. When I own the choices I've made that I regret, it gives me the freedom to take ownership also for the choices I made that I don't regret—the choices I made that have served my soul and helped me to grow, the courageous choices for living an authentic life.

Don't just take ownership of your mistakes and the things you regret doing or saying, or not doing or not saying. Take ownership of those good choices you made as well. Take ownership of the difficult choice to live authentically and not necessarily in agreement with others. Ownership is stepping into your personal power. There's no blame. There's no victim. There's no saboteur at work here, and there is no child involved. That little girl doesn't have to own anything. She was the one who was hurt. Ownership is for me, the adult: I am now taking ownership for my past actions, even those when I was a child or a teenager or a young adult or middle-aged, because I can bear the weight of ownership, because taking ownership gives me the freedom to release shame—and releasing shame leads me to compassion of self.

Compassion for Self

Compassion comes in all forms and has no price tag or expiration date. Compassion is the backbone of love, as it lifts you up and carries you and those around you through some of the darker times in life. Do not forget that you are human, that you will make mistakes, and that someone has shown you compassion at one time or another.

It is compassion that leads the way to forgiveness. It is compassion that leads the way to acceptance, and it is compassion that will lead the way to love—most importantly, love of yourself. How, you may ask, can I show compassion to myself? I know how to be compassionate with others around me, but how do I know I am being compassionate with myself? It is actually very simple. Any words you say to yourself, any actions you take that directly affect you, and any reactions you have that are or are not in alignment with your truth are opportunities for compassion.

Would you have compassion for someone with physical flaws? Would you have compassion for someone who mentally is not as intelligent or knowledgeable? Would you have compassion for people who have lost their way and seem to be surrounded by darkness, unable to find their own light? If the answer is yes, then you are capable of being compassionate toward others, and therefore toward yourself.

Show compassion to that part of yourself that dislikes your physical form, show compassion for that part of yourself that questions your own judgments or decisions, show compassion for that part of yourself that sometimes, despite what you know, does the very thing that hurts you the most. Show compassion for your own heart, and then you can show compassion for others through your own experiences, your own truths, and your own mistakes. Show compassion. *Be* compassion. Allow compassion into your life.

from *Daylight for the Soul* (2017/2021)

Chapter 5

Compassion

What is compassion? Is it feeling empathy for another human being? For mankind? For the planet? For yourself? It is all of the above. Having compassion is caring enough not only to feel something but also to do something. It is in the doing that one finds compassion. It is in the acting out and making a difference, in being there for someone or for your loved ones, for the planet, for yourself.

Compassion comes in many forms. It is the very essence of your soul, your spirit. A soul can soar, but only if there is compassion within. Ask yourself: have I been compassionate today? Have I truly cared for another or for myself? Have I acted in ways that showed that I cared instead of just thinking about it?

Many people might feel compassionate sitting on the couch and thinking about what they might do. But it is true compassion to get off the couch and actually be of service—service to mankind, to the planet, and to yourself.

You see, the first and most important person to have compassion for is *you*. Yes, you. How can you learn compassion, how important it is, if you do not feel it first with your heart and soul? If you do not show yourself grace, how can you show it to another? If you do not care for yourself, how can you care for another? How can you care for the planet? How can you save humanity?

We want compassion for ourselves, compassion for our loved ones, compassion for humankind, and compassion for the planet, in that order. So begin with yourself. Begin by giving yourself the compassion you need and deserve. Yes, you are worthy of compassion. Yes, you are worthy of love. Yes, you are worthy of the divine spark within you.

Compassion is the final step towards self-forgiveness. Have compassion for who you were; whether it was yesterday, a month ago, a year ago, or twenty years ago, and for where you were. Give grace, love, and compassion to that part of you that remains within. You are who you are now, so have compassion for who you were. Inside, you are every age you've ever been; you are every experience you've had and every memory, conscious or not. Every single word spoken or heard, every action against you or for you—every single memory of every single age you've ever been is contained within you.

Healing comes from having compassion for who you were at the time you said or didn't say, or did or didn't do, whatever it is you need and feel ready to be forgiven for. One way to have compassion for yourself is to picture yourself at that age; if your memory doesn't give you an image, look for an actual picture of yourself at that time. Even being around certain things —songs, smells, TV shows, or anything that evokes the feeling of that time period—can be help you picture who you were.

Having compassion for who you were results from a combination of awareness, acceptance, understanding, and ownership. Compassion is having self-love through acceptance. Isn't being accepting also being compassionate? Isn't the greatest act of compassion to be aware, to have acceptance, to understand

and love another? Why not love yourself with the same compassion you give to others?

If you are ready for self-forgiveness—and you are, or you would not be reading this—then you are ready to give yourself compassion. True compassion is compassion without conditions. Compassion is unconditional love. Compassion feels so pure that it takes you back to the beginning, when you were simply pure love at the beginning of your life. You still are! Pure love is still within you. That light has never been extinguished; pure love is still who you are inside. Compassion allows for your light to shine brighter so that you understand it is within your power to forgive yourself for anything you have done in your life. It is not about atonement, it is not about karma, it is not about punishment, it is simply about compassion. Love yourself enough to work through the steps of forgiveness so that you can get to the light of compassion.

Through awareness, you can be sorry for your actions; through acceptance, you can be sure in the knowledge that you cannot change the past; through understanding, you can know why you behaved the way you have in your life; and through ownership, you can be empowered by letting go of the victim and the saboteur. Compassion is loving your wholeness, loving your shadow and your light, loving every age you've ever been, allowing all those ages to be inside your heart and forgiving them all for anything that is still coming up for you to forgive.

These five steps can help you throughout your entire life. You can come back time and time again and go through these steps of self-forgiveness. No one else has to forgive you, as it is within your power to forgive yourself. It is compassionate to forgive. Forgiveness it is an act of compassion, and to love is to forgive. Forgiveness is the most powerful language of love on the planet. Why not give it to yourself? It is not just for others. It is most important for you, because when you have awareness, acceptance, understanding, ownership, and compassion, then and only then can you find forgiveness in loving all the parts of you.

My Personal Journey to Compassion

I am still on this journey as I move through all the steps of self-forgiveness. For me, that means not only having compassion for the adult I am now but for the child in me and every age and stage of my life: the teenage years, the young adult years, my thirties and forties, all the way to the fifty-eight-year-old person I am as I write this book. It is for the person I am right now, in this moment and in each moment moving forward. It is to have compassion for every single age within me, to understand the imperfections of this human life, to forgive myself and to forgive others, to choose to care and love myself above all others—not because I do not care about others or lack compassion for others, but because I must have compassion for myself first.

Therefore, I make choices that serve my soul and bring peace to my life, and that in turn enables me to be of service to others on their path to peace. Many of us, including me, were taught in this human life that we must put others before ourselves, but that is backwards: when I am serving myself from a place of love, I am filling myself up, and that cup then overflows to those around me so that I am truly able to be there for someone else. When I have compassion for myself, I can be completely compassionate with what others are going through. By first filling myself up with my own love and my own compassion, I have found that I am working from and towards a place of being whole and giving to others comes from a place of love and not obligation or fear.

I am a work in progress, and I always will be in this human life, as there is no perfection in being human. I am perfectly imperfect. I simply want to be in a place of awareness of self. I want to accept that I cannot change the past, and I want to accept who I am. I want to continue to understand my whys, and how those whys may change over time with healing and soul growth. I want to take ownership of all my words and actions and to take ownership of my thoughts and my feelings within myself too. And finally and most importantly, I want to have compassion for myself and in turn have compassion for all beings on this earth.

Conclusion

Forgiveness of Self

Self-forgiveness is the most important of all because you can forgive everyone around you and still not feel at peace. You can forgive others yet still feel unworthy of your own forgiveness. Self-forgiveness does not always come easily, and how you forgive yourself can be complicated. Even with the steps outlined in this book, it is and will be a unique process for everyone. For some of you, the steps of forgiveness will seemingly come easily as the words slip off your tongue. But do you truly believe what you are saying? This is the key—you must *believe* in the forgiveness you are giving. You must believe in your heart and soul that what you hold guilt, regret, and/or shame around *is* forgivable, and that you are empowered to forgive yourself. You can let go of the pain of the past and forgive. To forgive is to heal and to heal is to make peace with yourself.

Every one of you is worthy of forgiveness. You are pure love inside your soul, no matter what has happened, no matter what has been done or said or left undone or unsaid. You are worthy of love; and loving yourself means having compassion for every part of you. As you move through the steps of self-forgiveness to self-love, you will also find it easier to have more compassion for your neighbor and in turn for your community, for your country, and even more compassion for your planet. You see, forgiveness of self, and the pure love that is discovered and nourished in the process, will bring you to peace within yourself, and that peace within you will grow and touch everyone and everything around you.

Five Steps to Self-Forgiveness

Awareness that there is something to forgive

Acceptance that it cannot be
changed or undone

Understanding the "why" of
an action or inaction

Ownership of actions or inactions,
without justification

Compassion for who you were
then and who you are now

Importance of Self-Forgiveness

Before we can truly forgive another,
it is necessary to forgive ourselves.

Before we can truly accept and love ourselves,
it is necessary to forgive ourselves as we were.

Before we can truly forgive and love
ourselves, it is necessary to understand
our own words and actions.

Before we can truly forgive ourselves, it
is necessary to let go of the guilt, regret,
and shame that is rooted in fear.

Before we can truly be grounded
in the present, it is necessary to let
go of the past as the path to letting
go is through self-forgiveness.